MW00337295

SERMON-BOOSTER DRAMAS

by Tim Kurth

Loveland, Colorado

Acknowledgements

I offer special thanks to all the people who have brought my words to life, those who have made drama so effective in our worship. I thank also my entire congregation for embracing drama as an important element of worship. Finally, I would like to thank my family for the support they give me in all areas of ministry. Their names show up in many of these sketches.

Note:
The price of this book includes the right for you to make as many copies of the dramas you need for your immediate church performing group. If another church or organization wants copies of these dramas, it must purchase *Sermon–Booster Dramas* in order to receive performance rights.

Sermon-Booster Dramas

Copyright © 1997 Tim Kurth

All rights reserved. No part of this book may be reproduced in any manner whatsoever without prior written permission from the publisher, except as noted above and in the case of brief quotations embodied in critical articles and reviews. For information, write Permissions, Group Publishing, Inc., Dept. PD, P.O. Box 481, Loveland, CO 80539.

Credits
Editor: Bob Buller
Senior Editor: Michael D. Warden
Chief Creative Officer: Joani Schultz
Copy Editor: Julie Meiklejohn
Art Director: Lisa Chandler
Assistant Art Director: Kari K. Monson
Cover Art Director: Helen H. Lannis
Computer Graphic Artist: Joyce Douglas
Cover Designer: Paetzold Design
Production Manager: Gingar Kunkel

Library of Congress Cataloging-in-Publication Data
Kurth, Timothy J., 1958–
     Sermon-booster dramas / by Timothy J. Kurth.
         p.   cm.
     Includes index.
     ISBN 0-7644-2016-X
     1. Drama in public worship. 2. Drama in Christian education.
3. Christian drama, American. 4. Amateur plays.   I. Title.
BV289.K87   1997
246' .7–dc20

               96-44896
               CIP

10 9 8 7 6 5 4 3 2 1   06 05 04 03 02 01 00 99 98 97
Printed in the United States of America.

Contents

. . . .

Introduction

● ●

Using Drama in the Church

The stage is empty. There is nothing to suggest a place or a time. The actors, each with nothing more than a hat or a briefcase to suggest character, take the stage. Within two lines of dialogue you immediately connect with the setting and the characters. You know who they are and where they are, because you've been there yourself. You've heard the conversation. You know what they're feeling. And suddenly you're laughing or embarrassed or getting all choked up. All this in three minutes or less.

This was the magic of sketch comedy in the early days of television. The action was fast and furious when television was live and there were no second chances. From Milton Berle and Sid Caesar in the '50s to Sonny and Cher in the '70s, the television variety show lived and died by the three-minute sketch. People loved the characters on these shows. They knew them by heart. Jackie Gleason turned one sketch character, Ralph Kramden, into an American icon. It was this drama form that showed us how a little staging and a familiar face can touch our lives in the few minutes between commercials.

That's the inspiration for the sketches in this book. (In fact, that's why I call them sketches instead of skits.) However, we in the church have something so much more substantial to offer before and after the sketch than commercials. These sketches are written as sermon boosters. They set up the audience (the congregation) to hear the saving message of God's truth. There is no better reason to use drama in worship than to reveal the relationship people have with God through his Son, Jesus Christ. We want to captivate people with the message while remembering that we are not a part of the entertainment industry. To that end, this book is dedicated to helping people see God at work in their everyday lives.

In the next few pages, I hope to show you how to use drama in worship. You will understand this process best if you remember these simple principles of the sketch form:

● Establish mood and setting through dialogue.
● Use props only when they are necessary.
● Make the situations as broadly applicable as possible.
● Don't expect every issue to be resolved within the sketch.

One goal that I keep in mind when I write a sketch is to "get in and get out" as quickly as possible. When using drama in a worship setting, you must remember that the sketch is not the centerpiece. The dramatic sketch is a highlight. It evokes strong reactions from the audience. It sets the stage for a thought-provoking message. Often I've received more comments on the three-minute drama than on the thirty-minute sermon that followed. That is not to say, however, that the drama was more effective than the message. Rather, the drama encapsulated the message so clearly that people readily identified with it.

The dramas in this book are set in common, modern-day places, such as a backyard, an office, or a kitchen. One of my goals is for audience members to quickly connect a drama with their own experiences. Most of these dramas have only two characters because including more than two people requires greater character development before you can get to the point. This means more lines of dialogue to learn as well as more time to present the dialogue. When you include too many characters, you can lose the "punch" that a short sketch provides. The point of each of the dramas in this book is raised and dealt with quickly. Nearly every one has an element of humor as well as an element of challenge. Some are more humorous, others are more challenging. It's important to balance the two elements in a sketch, but in every case you'll want to conclude the sketch in such a way that the congregation is ready for what comes next; perhaps they'll be waiting for a question to be answered or a conflict to be resolved.

To help you connect a sketch to and integrate it with a sermon, I've included a number of relevant questions at the end of each sketch. These questions are intended to encourage people to identify with the characters, to stimulate thought before or after the sermon, to orient people to the sermon topic, and to help listeners apply the message of the drama and sermon to their everyday lives.

You can use the questions in a variety of ways. For example, you may ask congregation members to discuss one or more of the questions in pairs or small groups. However, if you sense that people might feel uncomfortable discussing certain questions, you may want to have them answer those questions silently before God. In addition, the pastor can pose a question at the beginning of the sermon to lead into the topic or at the end of the sermon to move people toward specific and concrete application of the topic.

I've been involved in theater since high school, both behind the scenes with set and lighting design and on stage. I love what happens when good actors, solid writing, and clever staging come together. Your drama presentations, however brief they might be, will have the greatest impact if they are well-presented. Here are some suggestions to help you in your preparations.

The Decision to Use Drama

You are probably holding this book because at some point, someone has considered adding drama to your worship services. Perhaps you're already using drama; maybe you're simply in the planning stages. The way you introduce drama into worship plays a crucial role in the way it is received. You must know your congregation. Some congregations will embrace launching full-scale weekly presentations from the start. Others may need to see drama work on special Sundays or have it introduced slowly (perhaps once a month or once a quarter) before they become comfortable with it.

At my church, we introduced drama through what we call our "contemporary service." This continues to be our dramas' home base, with occasional forays into the more traditional services or on special Sundays. The first drama actors were the senior pastor and myself. His involvement gave credibility to the use of drama in worship. It brought an almost instant comfort level to the congregation. Over time we've been able to develop a "troupe" of actors that enables us to vary the situations we can portray and broaden the scope of topics we can cover. No matter how you introduce drama into worship, you should seek to enhance the worship experience, not detract from it. Perhaps the most important key to accomplishing this is the wise selection of your players.

Building a Drama Troupe

Annual Christmas programs are probably the most common dramatic presentations in church. In these cases, we want to make sure that all the children are clearly visible to moms, dads, grandpas, grandmas, Aunt Esther, and Uncle Bob! So we give every child some role in the program, whether it's singing, speaking, or dressing up like an adorable sheep. This model is *not* the one we want to use for regular worship dramas! Please remember this simple truth: You'll find much more acting desire than acting talent in your congregation. Within your ranks are a few precious people who have the ability to command the stage. They will speak with confidence. They will "own" the scripted dialogue. They will understand their role as participants in a worship experience. Look for these people.

I'll probably err on the side of overemphasizing this point: Do not put just anyone on stage. At times I've been guilty of flinging open the doors of drama to anyone who was interested. I've cast people who were uncomfortable with their lines, spoke softly, could not face the audience, or had no sense of timing. When this happens, even a simple three-minute sketch will seem interminably long. Your drama team must be a small, handpicked group of individuals who understand their place within worship. They must commit to rehearsal times and memorizing the script. They must understand that the drama presentation is not about them or how well they present their lines. As important as good presentation is, the dramas must focus on God and our relationship with him. That's what makes them *worship* dramas.

Building a troupe needs to be a deliberate but not necessarily slow process. We started, as I said, with the pastor and myself. On very rare occasions (such as when one of us was out of town), we would invite one other person to perform. At first that person was our music director. As we discovered other talented actors, we nurtured their talents by inserting them into sketches on a more regular basis. We now have a core group of about a dozen players from age eight to adult. I rely on my players to schedule their own rehearsal time based on when the people performing that week can get together. However, you might want more formal rehearsal time with more supervision or direction. Do whatever works best for you.

Don't be afraid of using the same players too much. Good actors can play different characters each week without boring the congregation. You'll find that certain players are better at certain character types or stereotypes. This isn't a bad thing when it comes to short dramatic sketches. If you have several people who are really good at being what my twelve-year-old son calls the "clueless one," one of them can play that role whenever it comes up in a sketch. In fact, I'll let you in on a little secret. In most of these sketches, one of the characters is always a little clueless—sometimes aggressively so, sometimes comically so, and sometimes naively so. It's the character's lack of awareness that allows the other person to reveal the point to him or her (and to the audience).

You'll find, over time, that the audience will expect certain characters to behave in certain ways. You can take advantage of this in two ways: by meeting their expectations or by acting contrary to their expectations. Occasionally letting a stereotypically clueless character play a "wise teacher" role can add an element of surprise to the entire presentation. As with many things, a drama troupe will grow better with age as its members develop their individual and corporate talents more fully.

I ask actors to commit to the troupe for three or four months at a time. Once I have commitments, I select groupings of actors and the dates they will perform.

Most of my dramas use only two actors, so it's generally no problem to match people's schedules to our drama needs. When I receive the sermon topic for a specific Sunday from the pastor, I write the sketch for the people who are scheduled. Most of the sketches in this book contain the actual names of my drama troupe members who performed them originally. I would suggest that you replace the names in this book with the names of the actual people who perform the sketches in your church. This helps the actors, who don't have to remember another name, and the congregation, which identifies more easily with the players. Generally I finish each drama by Wednesday, we hold one rehearsal on Thursday or Saturday, and we perform on Sunday. However, you might want to modify my model in several ways.

First, you have all the sketches already on hand, so you don't need to write your own. Second, these are sermon-booster dramas, which means you'll want them to connect in some way to the sermons. Thus, your pastor will need to select sermon topics far enough in advance for you to build your drama schedule around them. It's unlikely that a pastor will set topics as far as four months in advance. However, if the pastor plans a series of sermons on the same topic or follows some other monthly schedule, that would be extremely helpful. Third, instead of scheduling specific people for specific dates far in advance, you might want to create a list of three or four "standby" actors for each week. Then when you select a drama, you can ask the people you'll need in that drama to perform that week. Make sure your standby group has enough people to cover any sketch you might select.

Staging a Dramatic Sketch

As I said in the opening, sketches are designed to be presented with little or no staging. Consequently, the placement of the actors, the way the actors come on stage, and the occasional use of sound effects are vitally important. You should also think about where the acting "platform" will be. In some churches, congregation members may find it unsettling to have a drama presented directly in front of the altar or baptismal area. If your facility permits it, select a neutral area that's clearly visible to the entire congregation. Our church has movable platforms in the front, with one section that's conveniently located between the pulpit and the band area. This section is slightly elevated for good visibility, and it has a blank wall behind it. We played around with a variety of presentation areas before settling on this as our primary drama location. The mobility of the platforms allows us to use different levels and easily manipulate the space for dramatic effect.

Actors can approach the stage from any location. Although most of the dramas in this book have directions to enter from stage left or stage right, these are merely suggestions so actors have a place to come from as they're entering the scene. Certain sketches are set within a church. "Hey, Dad!" (p. 36), for example, has a child approaching the stage from the congregation. In this case, the location from which the actor enters is a crucial part of the script.

When staging a sketch, instruct your actors to be "in character" the moment they become visible to the congregation. Also, novice actors have a tendency to face each other on stage as though they are holding a real conversation. Unfortunately, they turn their bodies away from the audience in the process. Stress to actors the importance of turning primarily toward the audience with only a suggestion of facing each other. This is called "three-quarters front." In other words, three-quarters of the front of an actor's body should be presented to the audience. Congregation members will lose interest in the sketch if they can't see the facial expressions and body language of the players.

In staging the few sketches that call for props, keep the props as simple as I have indicated. It takes very little to suggest a setting. In "Back in the Doghouse" (p. 14), for example, I suggest the watering of a suburban lawn with a hose by having Tim hold a simple spray nozzle. Invest the majority of your time in rehearsing lines and entrances. Polishing these elements will mean much more than collecting elaborate props.

Lighting and Sound

The beauty of these dramas is that they can be performed under various lighting conditions. (The only sketch in the book that requires special lighting is "While It Was Still Dark" [p. 71], a powerful Easter drama.) Our church lights are on breaker switches, so the lights are either on or off. Not long ago we added a few stage lights to brighten the altar and band area, but we've done nothing for dramatic effect specifically. Your main lighting concern should be to make sure your acting platform isn't noticeably darker than the other areas in front of the congregation.

Sound is another matter altogether. Quality sound is crucial to successful sketches. Drama is both a visual and an auditory experience. To create quality sound, you have several options. Churches with sufficient budgets and technical resources can equip the actors with wireless lavaliere microphones. For nearly all the sketches in this book, you will need only two microphones. In the early days of drama at my church, I would borrow the assistant pastor's microphone just before the sketch and return it to him as soon as I was finished. (If you borrow a pastor's microphone, always make sure you turn it off before returning it!)

A few sketches will require as many as four individual microphones. That's why I recommend having a single omnidirectional microphone on a boom stand. You can buy relatively inexpensive boom attachments for standard microphone stands. The microphone should be sensitive enough that the actors can be placed in natural positions and not have to speak directly into the microphone in order to be heard. The standard microphones used for singers or speakers are not sufficient. Whatever system you choose, make sure the sound can be turned on just before the action begins and turned off just after the sketch concludes.

Developing Your Own Dramas

At my church, we've made the commitment to weekly drama. It's always a challenge to prepare a fresh drama every week. You may not have the resources or the desire to present weekly dramas. Maybe you would rather present a new drama every other week or once a month.

No matter how often you use drama in your church, you can begin to develop and write your own material. Granted, it takes a good deal of creativity, but I'm certain God has blessed your congregation with people who have this talent. Look first to the members of your drama troupe. People who are excellent actors aren't always great writers, but you may find someone who has a flair for writing.

I find that the hardest part of creating a drama is coming up with the concept. After the pastor tells me the point of the message, I ask myself, "What common setting would best make or lead into this point?" Sometimes identifying the right setting is easy. Other times, several settings would work equally well. At times I've invited troupe members to participate in brainstorming sessions to develop settings and character types. I highly recommend this approach. It's difficult to write dialogue by committee, but developing concepts as a group can be a rewarding process.

Once I've determined the setting of the sketch and how the characters within the sketch relate to each other (they could be parents, siblings, co-workers, or friends, to list a few possibilities), I simply imagine the characters having a conversation. I'm always amazed at the path my characters take to get to the point. That may sound strange, but I've discovered that often a word or phrase I've written triggers another thought or response, and things take off. Eventually I get to the point, often more strongly than I had originally planned.

Try your hand at sketch development. Invite some creative people to look at several upcoming sermon topics and play around with dramatic interpretations of the sermons' main points. Draw on personal experience. Use conversations you've heard or had. At times I've been in situations in which people have turned to me and said, "This is going to end up in a sketch, isn't it?" Sometimes they've been right! I actually have a friend who punched out his windshield when his car broke down, just as the character named Mike did in "Something of Consequence" (p. 60). His name isn't Mike, but he was in the congregation the day we presented the sketch. He really connected with the message that day and was pleased that I could use his experience to make a point.

When writing a sketch, remember your goal: to "get in and get out" quickly. One or two lines of introductory dialogue is all you have time for. Indicate location or relationship with those lines or with very simple props. For example, a table, a glass of water, and one person telling another, "I was waiting to order until you got here," immediately sets the scene in a restaurant. You can now move right to the point of the sketch. The next lines should introduce the problem or conflict. One person can state a concern or have it drawn out by the other character. Once the concern is clear, you'll want to bring the sketch to a conclusion. There is no need to resolve every issue. The sketch may conclude by reinforcing the concern or problem so that the sermon can pick up from the ending of the sketch. The last line or two should be a "punch line" that evokes some response from the audience. Whether audience members laugh, are taken by surprise, or are left deep in thought, the pastor can seize this moment to create the best effect.

I encourage you to try your hand at sketch development and writing. Not only will you have more drama options, you'll also be able to address situations and issues specific to your congregation or location. I recently wrote a dramatic sketch that highlighted our congregation's twenty-fifth anniversary. I've also written sketches with references to the Bears or the Bulls because our church is located near Chicago. All these things help speed the connections your people make to the sketch and to its message.

I'm pleased to share the sketches in this book with you. Our congregation has benefited greatly from the use of these dramas, and it's wonderful that they can be used to enhance worship elsewhere. When I started writing dramas for worship, I never intended to release them publicly. But God has opened the door for me to reach others with these scripts. I pray that he will bless your ministry and the message you present at the end of each drama!

Am I Wrong?

Themes: Guilt, pride, sin

Characters: Brad, a middle manager in an office; Kerby, one of Brad's co-workers

Setting: The hallway of an office just outside of a meeting room

Prop: A file folder full of papers

Message: All too often, our pride prevents us from confronting problems we have created. We would rather excuse our behavior than do what it takes to repair a situation. Our pride separates us from each other. It is also at the heart of what separates us from God.

(Brad enters from stage left, carrying a file folder full of papers. He is walking briskly and seems irritated. Kerby follows closely behind him while she says her first line. She should overtake Brad at center stage.)

Kerby: Brad! Hey, Brad. Come back here.

Brad: Do you mind, Kerby? I just want to be left alone.

Kerby: I don't think you mean that.

Brad: Of course I mean it. Leave me alone!

Kerby: Brad, I really need to talk to you. You know, you really made a mess of things back there.

Brad: Me? Me? Why is it always me? Why are you blaming me for the mess?

Kerby: Oh, I don't know. Could it be that you were in charge? that you didn't do your job? that the whole project was your idea from start to finish? *(Pauses.)* And what a finish! It could take us weeks to dig ourselves out of the hole you've gotten us into.

Brad: *(Defensively)* You're just looking for a scapegoat—someone you can hang out to dry when things heat up. Well, I'll tell you right now—it's not going to be me!

Kerby: Brad, there's not going to be any "hanging out to dry" here. But if you're talking about who's responsible . . . it *is* you! You were wrong. You blew this one.

Brad: I wouldn't go that far.

Kerby: You never go that far.

Brad: What do you mean by that?

Kerby: What I mean is that I hardly ever hear you admit that you're wrong. You always have some sort of excuse. *(Mimicking Brad)* "I thought someone else was taking care of that." "You misunderstood me." "That's just your perception." You know, it drives everyone in the office a little crazy.

Brad: Oh, so now everybody thinks I'm wr . . .

Kerby: See, you can't even say the word! Come on, sound it out . . . w-r-o-n-g.

Brad: Why are you harassing me like this?

Kerby: You mean besides just for fun?

> *(Brad turns to walk away.)*

Kerby: Wait, I'm sorry. That was a mean thing to say.

> *(Brad turns around.)*

Kerby: I'm bugging you about this because I think you need to know how difficult it is to work with someone who thinks he can never be wrong. We all know that you're human and that every human makes mistakes. Admitting that you've made a mistake isn't a sign of weakness. But when you won't admit you're wrong, it only makes matters worse. It really strains relationships around here. Haven't you noticed?

Brad: Well, sometimes people do seem to go out of their way to avoid me. I thought maybe it was my cologne!

Kerby: Brad, I'm serious. Admitting your mistakes and sharing your weaknesses gives us a chance to support you. It allows all of us to work together as a team so that everyone can benefit. But as long as you keep pretending that nothing's wrong . . . well, it makes the situation worse for all of us.

Brad: But saying I'm . . . you know . . . is like admitting I don't know what I'm doing. It makes me feel incompetent and unnecessary. It feels like I'm telling the whole world I'm a failure. Everyone will laugh at me.

Kerby: Wow! That's a truckload of baggage you're carrying around there. Saying you're wrong doesn't mean any of those things. I think it means that you're sharp, savvy, able to see when a mistake has been made, smart enough to learn from it, and strong enough to move beyond it. I don't know who's been sneaking those negative messages into your head, but I'd tell them to shut up if I were you.

Brad: *(Pauses thoughtfully.)* Thanks, Kerby. You've given me a lot to think about. This isn't going to be easy, but I can see how it will help with the whole mess all around. I hope everyone will give me a second chance.

Kerby: And a third, and a fourth…Hey, we're all in this together. Now come on, let's get back in there and straighten this thing out.

Brad: All right. *(Brightening)* You know, I was sure that this plan was going to work. I guess I was…well…not right!

Discussion Questions:

● When was the last time you admitted you were wrong? How did it feel?

● What makes it hard for you to recognize your mistakes? to admit them?

● When have you confronted someone who was wrong? How did that person react?

● How do you react when you do something wrong? when someone else does something wrong?

Back in the Doghouse

· ·

Themes: God's character, love

Characters: Tim, a worried husband; Brad, a helpful
neighbor

Setting: The front lawn of a suburban home

Prop: A spray nozzle that fits a garden hose

Message: Although many of us recognize that God's love
for us is unconditional, we still tend to feel that we're
responsible to make ourselves lovable. This is most evi-
dent in our relationships with others. We put pressure
on ourselves to always "do the right thing" and prove to
others that we're worthy of their love. Unfortunately,
when we act this way, we often rob ourselves of the joy
that true love can bring.

*(Tim, standing center stage and holding a spray nozzle, pretends to water the
lawn. No hose needs to be attached. Brad enters from stage left.)*

Brad: Hey, Tim—what's going on?

Tim: *(Holding the nozzle in one position the entire time)* Just watering my lawn.
It's been a long, dry summer, you know.

Brad: Just watering the lawn, huh? Are you sure there's not something else on
your mind?

Tim: Can't a guy water his lawn without there being some deeper meaning to it?
What makes you think I've got something on my mind?

Brad: Well, for starters, you haven't moved that nozzle since I came out three
minutes ago. You're doing such a wonderful job of watering that four-by-four

patch that I think your lawn is starting to run down the sidewalk.

Tim: *(Lowering the nozzle suddenly to show he's stopped spraying)* Oh! OK, so maybe I am a little preoccupied. *(Pauses.)* I think I'm in the doghouse.

Brad: *(Laughing)* Again?

Tim: I'm serious. I have a funny feeling that I'm in trouble with my wife. What's worse, I can't figure out what I could have done wrong.

Brad: What makes you think you're in trouble?

Tim: Well, it's my birthday…

Brad: Happy birthday!

Tim: Thanks. Usually Elizabeth does something special for my birthday. But this year…nothing. I'm just sure I did something to hurt her feelings. I'm out here trying to figure out what it was.

Brad: Maybe it's a surprise.

Tim: What—the birthday…or what I did to make her mad?

Brad: The birthday, obviously.

Tim: That's not it. Elizabeth can't keep secrets very well. I've always been able to find them out. No, there's got to be something else.

Brad: *(Jokingly)* Then maybe she doesn't love you anymore.

Tim: *(Seriously)* Do you think that's it? I knew it! I've done something so bad that she doesn't love me anymore.

Brad: Get a grip, Tim! I was joking. Surely you don't think you could do something that would make her stop loving you—especially something you can't even remember.

Tim: Don't be so sure. In my experience, love can come and go pretty quickly. Sometimes you do something stupid and Bang! It's gone!

Brad: So what do you do to keep this from happening?

Tim: I always try to be on my best behavior, to be as lovable as I possibly can.

Brad: You never have a bad day? You don't have moments when you're unlovable?

Tim: I sure try not to when I'm around others.

Brad: Tim, you can't make people love you.

Tim: That may be true, but I always try my best not to upset anyone. I do what I can to please everyone.

Brad: That sounds like an awful lot of work. Does this make you happy?

Tim: I didn't say I wanted to be happy, Brad. I just want to be loved.

Discussion Questions:

- Have you ever tried to earn other people's love? Why or why not?
- In what ways have you tried to earn other people's love? God's love?
- In what ways might you make others feel that they must earn your love?
- What are the benefits of trying to please others? What are the dangers?
- If you were Brad, how would you help Tim realize that he can't earn love?

Branching Out

· ·

Themes: Commitment, faith

> **Characters:** Remaining Branch; Rebelling Branch
>
> **Setting:** A vineyard
>
> **Prop:** A pole, a hat tree, or a microphone stand
>
> **Message:** Based on John 15, this drama presents a conversation between two branches that are connected to a vine. The Remaining Branch represents those who understand that being connected to God is vital for survival. The Rebelling Branch represents those who strive for independence from God, not recognizing that this means certain death.

(The two Branches stand center stage and hold on to the pole, which represents the vine. The Remaining Branch should stay calm and composed throughout the sketch. The Rebelling Branch, tired of connection and dependence, is anxious to move on and should act agitated throughout the sketch.)

Rebelling: *(Animatedly)* How can you *do* that?

Remaining: *(Calmly)* What exactly am I doing?

Rebelling: Go ahead. Pretend you don't know. *(Pauses.)* How can you hang there so calm and composed? You barely move.

Remaining: I'm a branch. I'm connected to this vine *(gesturing to the vine)*. Moving about freely isn't a high priority for me. I'm quite content simply to remain here.

Rebelling: Not me, buddy. I am tired of being dependent on this vine. Every day it's the same thing. The vine feeds us, the vine keeps us together, the vine makes us larger and stronger.

Remaining: And this is a bad thing?

Rebelling: I'm not saying it's a bad thing. It's just that I want to take care of myself. I want to make my own decisions. I want to set my own course.

Remaining: That is the most ridiculous thing I have ever heard. You know what happens to branches that leave the vine.

Rebelling: Rumors and propaganda! I've heard the scary bedtime stories about withering and dying, but I don't believe them for a second. I think they're vine scare-tactics to keep us from exploring life for ourselves. Listen—there's a big, exciting world out there, and we're missing it because we're stuck to this vine.

Remaining: So you want to strike out on your own, make your mark on the world, carve out a niche for yourself, become a self-made branch.

Rebelling: *(Excitedly)* Now you've got it! That's exactly what I want.

Remaining: Well, what you want is simply ridiculous.

Rebelling: *(With building frustration)* There is nothing ridiculous about wanting to set my own course, make my own way, experience life. But that is simply not going to happen as long as I am stuck here. *(Pauses.)* I suppose you're happy just to . . . to . . .

Remaining: To remain.

Rebelling: What?

Remaining: To remain. I'm happy simply to remain. You may think that it's just a rumor, but I believe that apart from this vine I *will* wither and die. Besides, even if that risk weren't there, I'd be happy to be connected to something that feeds, strengthens, and cares for me. Look around you. See all of the other branches? What would you do off on your own?

Rebelling: I would explore. I'd make my own way. When I was hungry I'd attach myself to the nearest tree or bush, stick *(snickering at his own pun)* around for a while, and move along whenever I felt like it. I'd make new friends of my own choosing. Maybe they wouldn't even be branches!

Remaining: I'm sorry to see you so restless. I guess there's nothing that will change your mind. You know the vine won't stop you if you choose to break away, but we're all going to miss you.

Rebelling: *(Beginning to struggle against the vine)* Don't think you can get me to stay by using that sappy sentimentality. You won't miss me so much. Besides, I'm sure my travels will bring me back this way someday.

Remaining: I certainly hope you'll have that chance.

(The Rebelling Branch is now struggling too hard to talk. Finally the Branch breaks free, takes one or two steps from the vine, and collapses to the floor.)

Discussion Questions:

- With which of the characters do you identify most closely and why?

- What are the dangers of trying to make our own way? What might be some benefits?

- What are the benefits of depending entirely on Jesus? What might be some dangers?

- When do you most feel like breaking away from God's vine, Jesus?

- What can you do during the coming week to depend on Jesus more?

Christmas Coma

• •

Themes: Busyness, Christmas

Characters: Pamela, a confused Christmas shopper; Rex, a concerned friend

Setting: A street corner

Props: Several shopping bags full of items

Message: When our focus shifts from the Christ child to the Christmas rush, the holiday season can completely overwhelm us and sensory overload can shut us down. This is not a problem just during the Christmas season. It's a risk we take any time we try to manage our lives apart from our relationship with God.

(The sketch opens with Pamela holding the shopping bags and staring blankly into space. She is motionless. Rex enters from stage left and calls to her.)

Rex: Hi, Pamela. *(No response)* Pamela? *(Moves closer.)* Pamela? *(Waves his hand in front of Pamela's face.)* Pamela, you're scaring me! *(Shakes Pamela's shoulder gently.)* Pamela, are you all right?

Pamela: *(Coming to with a start)* No, I think the red ribbon looks better with that package... *(seeing Rex)* Oh—hi, Rex. Where did you come from?

Rex: I've been here for a while. And in case you hadn't noticed, there's no package or red ribbon anywhere in sight. Pamela, we're standing on a street corner.

Pamela: *(Slightly embarrassed)* I know where we are. I was simply reviewing my wrapping designs for when I get home.

Rex: Nice try. But when I walked up a minute ago, you were nearly catatonic. I was just about to call 911.

Pamela: OK, you caught me at my holiday worst. This happens every year. I call it my Christmas coma. I've literally lost days out of my life because of it. One year I remember going into a mall on Monday, and the next thing I knew, I was at the office party on Friday night. Usually it doesn't happen quite so publicly. I try to get home before it hits.

Rex: Well, you didn't quite make it this time. Do you need some help?

Pamela: I just need the holidays to be over. If I get one more party invitation or have to find a parking spot at one more mall, you may have to have me institutionalized.

Rex: *(Playfully)* Is it safe to assume that you're not experiencing the peace and joy of this blessed holiday season?

Pamela: You're very perceptive. This blessed holiday season is the biggest burden of the year. I'm no Scrooge, but if someone decided to cancel Christmas, you wouldn't find me complaining! The strangest thing is that every year around Thanksgiving, I actually look forward to this season. Maybe my coma causes amnesia!

Rex: Before you become a hypochondriac, maybe it's time to free yourself from the tinsel and trappings of Christmas and get back to the basics. We've turned up the volume on this holiday to the point that we can't even hear the still, small voice of the baby born in Bethlehem.

Pamela: That describes me perfectly. Unfortunately, the only thing I can hear right now is the Muzak version of "Joy to the World!" over and over and over again. Maybe that's why by the time Christmas actually gets here, all I want to do is crawl into bed for about a week.

Rex: If you ask me, Christmas is just the climax of 365 days of an overcommitted and overwhelming lifestyle. I'm not pretending to be much better off than you. We all need a little time and freedom to find the peace that was promised two thousand years ago.

Pamela: I'm with you. I just wish I knew where to start. *(Pauses.)* I can tell you one thing—it's certainly not at the mall. I should know. I've been to every store!

Discussion Questions:

- What causes you to lose sight of the real meaning of Christmas?
- If you could describe a perfect Christmas, what would it look like?
- What could you do this week to help create your perfect Christmas?
- What can you do now to avoid becoming overwhelmed by Christmas?

Do the Right Thing

....

Themes: Busyness, time management

Characters: Brad, a talented musician; Tim, a sound technician and a friend of Brad's

Setting: Immediately after a music rehearsal

Props: A microphone with a cable and several musical instruments such as keyboards or guitars

Message: Having a talent can be a blessing, but it can also be a challenge. It's flattering when people recognize our gifts, but it can lead to disaster. In fact, an inability to say no and a tendency to overcommit when others want us to use our talents often lead to stress and the eventual collapse of our effectiveness.

Production note: Since the setting is a praise and worship rehearsal, the character of Brad might best be played by your church's music leader.

(Brad is seated center stage behind a keyboard [or holding a guitar]. Tim is slightly left of center stage, coiling a microphone cable as though he is tearing down after a music rehearsal.)

Tim: Hey, Brad—you did a great job with last week's African Missions Festival.

Brad: Thanks, Tim. I thought it went well.

Tim: "Went well" is the norm for you, but this was exceptional even by your standards! In fact, I hear through the grapevine that some people *really* enjoyed it.

Brad: I hope everyone enjoyed it! *(Pauses.)* You haven't heard anything negative, have you?

Tim: Not one word. What I meant was that I've heard that some people enjoyed it enough to ask you to do some extra work for them—a concert, maybe some recording. Or are these just wild rumors?

Brad: No, you heard right. I have been invited to take on a couple of extra projects.

Tim: You know, I don't mean to stick my nose into your life—but do you think that's wise?

Brad: What do you mean?

Tim: Well, just because people are impressed with you and want you to do something for them, does that mean you should do it? I'm just wondering if it's right to let others push you into things.

Brad: Hold on, hold on! Nobody's pushing me into anything. I happen to be the right person for them, and this is an exciting opportunity. I can do a good job, and it shouldn't take *that* long to do what they've asked. Besides, I don't want to let anyone down.

Tim: Brad, you're dodging the issue. Whether you're the right person or whether you can fit it into your schedule isn't the point. I asked if it was the right thing to do.

Brad: I'm not dodging the point, but I am missing it. If I'm in a position to do what they've asked and I can find the time to do it, why shouldn't I?

Tim: Now you're pulling my leg. You can't seriously be asking me that question.

Brad: Of course I'm serious—since you're so smart, tell me how doing this isn't right.

Tim: OK, you asked for it. First, you've been saying how busy you've been lately and how you miss spending time with your family, right?

Brad: OK...go on.

Tim: And just the other day, you were complaining that it's getting harder and harder for you to find time for yourself—time to relax and recharge your batteries.

Brad: All right, enough already! I get the point. You think I should just tell people no. I should disappoint everyone by refusing to do what I'm capable of doing.

Tim: Perhaps you already are disappointing them. In fact, I'm going to go out on a limb and guess that you may even be disappointing yourself.

Brad: Listen, Tim—I just want to do the right thing and have everyone be happy with me.

Tim: Which one?

Brad: What?

Tim: Which one? Do you want to do the right thing, or do you want everyone to be happy with you? Sometimes you can truly accomplish only one of the two.

Discussion Questions:

- To what extent is it possible to do the right thing and to please everyone?

- What are the dangers of always trying to do what other people ask?

- When might doing the right thing *require* you to disappoint people?

- How can we know when we should do what others ask? tell them no?

- In what areas of your life are you overcommitted? undercommitted?

Dropping Anchor

Themes: Disappointment, hope

Characters: Rex, a disappointed man; Pamela, a supportive but confused friend

Setting: A restaurant at lunch time

Props: A small table, two chairs, and a glass of water

Message: It's not unusual for us to anchor our hopes on various things. But problems occur when "things" shift and leave us disappointed. With no solid anchor in our lives, we can become discouraged and even hopeless. But when we anchor ourselves on God and his promises, he will never disappoint us.

(Rex is seated at a table playing distractedly with a glass of water. Pamela enters stage left to join Rex.)

Pamela: Hi, Rex. I hope you haven't waited long.

Rex: *(Unenthusiastically)* Not long.

Pamela: Thanks for inviting me to lunch. I must admit it was a surprise. What's the occasion?

Rex: No occasion.

Pamela: *(Somewhat confused)* What's going on, Rex? You seemed much more chipper when you called this morning.

Rex: That was this morning. A lot can happen in a few hours, if you know what I mean.

Pamela: Frankly, I'm a little lost. I was anticipating good news.

Rex: So was I! I was hoping to take the afternoon off.

Pamela: *(Brightening)* That would be great! It's a beautiful day. Are you going to go fishing or just lie in the sun?

Rex: Actually, I was hoping to go out and shop for a new television.

Pamela: Having seen your old one, I would say that's a good idea.

Rex: Then I was hoping to stop by a couple of car lots and start looking for a new car.

Pamela: *(Excitedly)* Rex, that sounds fantastic! *(Pauses, slightly deflated.)* Now I'm totally confused.

Rex: Tell me about it.

Pamela: No—I mean it. Everything that you're doing today sounds fun and exciting. But you're as down as I've ever seen you.

Rex: Pamela, I don't think you were listening. I didn't say I was *doing* those things today. I said I was *hoping* to do those things today. But all my plans fell apart, and now I'm feeling kind of adrift.

Pamela: How could things change so quickly?

Rex: I anchored all my plans on one big hope. To be honest, I wanted it to be more than a hope. I was absolutely certain that I was getting a promotion and a big raise today. I planned on it.

Pamela: And it didn't happen.

Rex: I'll say. I got a tiny plaque thanking me for five years of faithful service and a twenty-dollar gift certificate to this restaurant. I guess I shouldn't complain—at least I can pay for lunch.

Pamela: I'm sorry, Rex. *(Pauses.)* Maybe I shouldn't say anything, but it sounds as though you dropped anchor in the wrong place.

Rex: It feels as though the anchor dropped on me instead!

Pamela: Well, that would explain why you're feeling so crushed.

Discussion Questions:

● When have you anchored your hopes on something that disappointed you?

● On what or whom are you anchoring your hopes right now?

● To what extent is it possible to completely avoid feeling disappointed?

● What can we do to limit disappointment in our lives? to overcome it?

Gardening

· · · · · · · · · · · · · · · · · · ·

Themes: Jesus, loneliness

Characters: Kerby, a lonely single woman; Lana, an acquaintance

Setting: A coffee shop

Props: A small circular table, two chairs, a cup of coffee, and a magazine

Message: Busy lives and constant activity do not protect us from loneliness. Although it's sometimes difficult to cope with feelings of loneliness, there is comfort in knowing that Jesus experienced life fully as a human. He knows our feelings intimately and cares for us even in our loneliest moments.

(Kerby is seated at a small circular table center stage. There is a cup of coffee in front of her, and she is flipping distractedly through a magazine. Lana enters from stage left.)

Lana: Hey, Kerby! *(Pauses, then touches Kerby on the shoulder.)* Kerby?

Kerby: *(Startled)* What?! Oh—hi, Lana. You startled me!

Lana: I'm sorry—I didn't mean to sneak up on you. Are you all alone?

Kerby: *(Defensively)* Why would you ask a question like that?

Lana: Well...there's no one else sitting with you. It seemed like a fairly straight-forward question to ask.

Kerby: Oh, I'm sorry! You really were just asking if I was by myself.

Lana: Should I go away and come back again? You seem really out of it!

Kerby: No, don't go. It's just that your question about being "alone" struck a nerve. I was just sitting here thinking about how alone I really am.

Lana: *(Sitting down)* What's going on?

Kerby: Well, I just started a new job...

Lana: I know. I thought everything was going great.

Kerby: It is, but I haven't really gotten to know anyone there yet. My job doesn't require a lot of interaction with people, so I think it's going to take a long time to develop new friendships.

Lana: You're probably right, but it shouldn't take *that* long to get acquainted. In the meantime, you've got other friends, don't you?

Kerby: Yeah, but I'm beginning to realize that just about all my current friends are from my old job. Most of my time with them was spent doing business stuff. On top of that, I live alone, and my cat's not such a great conversationalist.

Lana: Sounds like you're pretty lonely.

Kerby: I am—lonely and scared to death.

Lana: Scared? I must be in a different place than you. I like it when I can find time alone.

Kerby: Lana, I'm not talking about time alone. I'm talking about loneliness. It's this dark feeling that I'm unlovable. I go nuts thinking I may never find another friend, that sooner or later everyone will desert me. No one wants to go where I'm going; no one wants to do what I'm doing. Sometimes it gets so bad that *I* don't even want to go where I'm going or do what I'm doing.

Lana: Sounds like you could spend some time in the garden.

Kerby: What are you talking about? I'm sharing my pain, and you want to talk botany!

Lana: That's not it at all. When you said that no one wants to go where you go or do what you do, I thought of Jesus. I know it's hard to be alone, but Jesus knows it better than anyone else. His night in the Garden was pretty traumatic... and desperately lonely. Maybe no one else can really know what you're feeling right now, but I guarantee that Jesus does.

Kerby: I understand what you're saying, and I appreciate the thought, but even knowing that Jesus went through the same thing and knows how I feel doesn't make it hurt any less. I'm glad he's there to empathize, but I sure hope this loneliness passes quickly.

Lana: I think in his loneliest moments, that's what Jesus wished for, too.

Kerby: You're probably right. *(Pauses.)* Well, I guess the only thing I can do right now is to take up gardening!

Discussion Questions:

- How is Kerby's loneliness like Jesus' loneliness? How is it different?

- What do you think causes some people to be lonelier than others?

- How do you think Jesus coped with his loneliness in the Garden?

- What steps would you take to help Kerby cope with her loneliness?

- What can you do this week to avoid feeling lonely? to help someone else not feel lonely?

Godly Women

· ·

Themes: Mother's Day, women

Characters: Tim, an avid golfer; Brad, Tim's neighbor

Setting: Early Sunday morning in a suburban neighborhood

Props: A golf bag and golf clubs

Message: Mother's Day is not an official church holiday. However, it is a good reminder that we need to take time to honor the women in our lives.

(Tim crosses the stage carrying his golf bag and golf clubs. He passes Brad, who is standing center stage.)

Brad: Hey, Tim—where ya going?

Tim: *(Pausing to look at his clubs, then sarcastically)* I'm going fishing, Brad . . . what does it look like?

Brad: I didn't literally mean, "Where are you going?" I meant why are you going out golfing today?

Tim: Why not? It's Sunday, I'm not working, and for once it seems that the weather forecast was right! I'm going golfing. Are you upset that I didn't invite you?

Brad: Tim, it's Mother's Day. Don't you think it's a little insensitive to go golfing by yourself on Mother's Day?

Tim: Oh, I understand your problem. Listen, Brad—my mom died several years ago, so I really don't pay much attention to this little "Hallmark holiday" these days.

Brad: What about your wife?

Tim: *(Incredulously)* She's not my mother.

Brad: You're a total pig, aren't you?

Tim: Why are you so worked up about this, buddy? *(Mockingly)* Is your wife making you stay home and spend time with her today?

Brad: I was wrong—"pig" was far too complimentary!

Tim: Get over it, Brad. This is a make-believe holiday to sell greeting cards.

Brad: You may have a point. It is very commercial. Still, you need to honor the women in your life.

Tim: What are you talking about?

Brad: This may be a manufactured holiday, but if someone didn't slow us down a little and remind us to honor women, I'm afraid we'd all go off to the golf course and never stop to think about what a gift God has given us.

Tim: I was just wondering, Brad . . . does your wife ever let you out to play?

Brad: Well, I'm wondering when you take time to let your wife know how important she is to you. And not just your wife, but your daughter, your sister, and all women, whether they're mothers or wives or not.

Tim: You watch a lot of daytime talk shows, don't you?

Brad: I can see you're not taking this very seriously.

Tim: Don't be mad. I appreciate the sentiment, and you *have* given me something to think about. In fact, I think I'll pick up a card on my way home. But right now, I've got to get going, or I'll miss my tee time.

Discussion Questions:

- Who has been the most important female in your life and why?
- What have you done to show that person how much she means to you?
- Why do you think women sometimes feel unappreciated in the home? in the church?
- What can you do to honor the women in your life during the coming week? every day?

Happy Valentine's Day

....

Themes: Love, relationships, Valentine's Day

Characters: Rex, a rather grumpy middle-aged man; Brad, a friend

Setting: A chance post-Valentine's Day meeting

Props: None needed

Message: Sharing love entails vulnerability and risk. God risked everything, even his Son, to demonstrate his love for us. However, we're reluctant to share love with others because we fear rejection and hurt. God calls us to take that risk so that everyone might know his love.

(Rex enters from stage right and crosses as Brad enters from stage left. They meet center stage.)

Brad: Hi, Rex.

Rex: Hey, Brad—it's good to see you.

Brad: Thanks—it's good to see you, too. Did you have a great Valentine's Day?

Rex: Not particularly. I don't go for all those overhyped holidays the greeting card companies create.

Brad: Didn't get any cards again this year, huh?

Rex: Nope!

Brad: Didn't send any cards again this year, either?

Rex: Nope! I saved the postage and treated myself to lunch.

Brad: I don't understand you, Rex. I've never met anyone who's so sour about Valentine's Day.

Rex: Well, excuse me if I don't go for all that sappy "Be My Valentine" artificial love. I don't let my emotions run away with me.

Brad: Who says that sharing a caring thought or expression of love is artificial just because you do it on Valentine's Day? Surely there's someone you care about and want to show love to.

Rex: Actually, I try to avoid that as much as I can. There's just too much risk involved. Taking myself to lunch is a far safer bet!

Brad: Risk? I'm missing something here.

Rex: What's to miss? You start caring for someone, and that leads to a relationship. Relationships lead to commitment, and commitment makes you vulnerable. There you have it—risk.

Brad: What about the rewards, though?

Rex: Oh, I suppose you're talking about someone who cares about me, will be there when I'm down, help me when I'm sick, watch out for all my needs, that kind of thing.

Brad: Yeah, that kind of thing was exactly what I was talking about. Aren't those rewards?

Rex: Maybe in the short term. But it never lasts. Things fall apart. Angry words are exchanged. People leave. *(Sadly, slowly)* People always leave.

Brad: Do you really think that?

Rex: I don't just think it—I speak from experience. Listen, Brad—I'm a self-made man. I can fend for myself and meet my own needs. I don't want or need anyone to care for, and I certainly don't need anyone to care for me.

Brad: Well, that pretty much explains your Valentine's Day attitude.

Rex: Oh—it does, does it?

Brad: Yep! No risk, no relationship; no relationship, no reward; no reward, no... *(shrugs)* well, happy Valentine's Day!

Discussion Questions:

- To what extent do you agree with Rex? disagree with him?
- What do you think are the risks of loving someone? of not loving?
- How would you convince Rex that the reward of loving is worth the risk?
- Which is more rewarding: to love or to be loved? Which is more important?
- What are the three greatest rewards you have gained from loving? from being loved?

Heaven-Bound Express

· · · · · · · · · · · · · · ·

Themes: Bible study, eternal life

Characters: Jason, a man who is waiting for a train; Laura, a stranger who is also on the train platform

Setting: A train platform

Props: None needed

Message: Many people place their hope in God. They hope that there is a God and that they know enough about him to get to heaven. Behind these hopes, however, lies very little real understanding. Much like someone waiting for a train without checking the schedule, people hope in and wait on God without taking the time to check out his Word.

(Jason is standing center stage. Laura approaches him from stage right.)

Laura: Excuse me.

Jason: Yes?

Laura: Are you waiting for a train?

Jason: Yep! The Heaven-Bound Express.

Laura: Great! Then I'm in the right place.

Jason: I sure hope so. Do you want to board the Express too?

Laura: That's the plan. *(Pauses.)* Did you say you hope we're in the right place?

Jason: Well—yes, I did. I just hope I'm on the right platform.

Laura: Well, when is this train arriving? You see, I called and got all the information, but I lost that slip of paper.

Jason: The train will get here . . . soon . . . I hope.

Laura: Maybe I'm asking the wrong person. You seem to be doing an awful lot of hoping. Don't you know anything for sure?

Jason: *(Glibly)* I'm sure hoping.

Laura: *(Irritably)* Stop that! Don't you have a schedule or something? There's no one at the window, and there's no schedule posted anywhere.

Jason: Don't be silly. Of course I have a schedule. *(Pointing)* It's right over there in my bag.

Laura: *(Calmer, taking a deep breath)* That's better. So you do know when to expect the train?

Jason: Why do you say that?

Laura: You said you had a schedule, so you must know when the train arrives.

Jason: Oh, you're assuming I know what the schedule says.

Laura: You haven't looked at the schedule?

Jason: I didn't say that. I glanced at it. It was pretty hard to understand, but I'm pretty sure I'm on the right track.

Laura: So you really haven't studied the schedule.

Jason: That would take a lot of time and effort, don't you think?

Laura: Let me get this straight. You haven't studied the schedule, so you don't know if you're on the right platform or even if the train will arrive, yet you still expect to board the Heaven-Bound Express?

Jason: I sure hope so.

Discussion Questions:

- How accurately does this sketch depict non-Christians? Christians?
- How would you respond if someone asked you how to get to heaven?
- How, if at all, can anyone be sure that he or she is bound for heaven?
- What do you think most people are trusting to get them to heaven?

Hey, Dad!

· · · · · · · · · · · · · · · ·

Themes: Family, parenting, prayer

Characters: Dad, a worship leader; Jesse, his eleven-year-old son

Setting: The church during a worship service

Props: None needed

Message: Prayer can be difficult if we approach it as mystical contact with a faraway being. It's much easier to pray if we can see God as our "daddy" and ourselves as his children.

Production note: This sketch can be set up as a surprise. The players can be the actual worship leader, who would normally be stepping up to lead a section of the service, and his or her child. Be sure to change the names of the characters to match your situation.

(Dad steps up as if to continue leading the service. Jesse comes from a seat in one of the front rows of the congregation and calls to him. Jesse should act completely unaware of the congregation.)

Jesse: Hey, Dad?

Dad: Jesse, I don't think this is such a good time.

Jesse: Oh—*(glances over his shoulder and notices that he has interrupted)* sorry, but this will only take a minute.

Dad: All right, but we'll have to make it quick. We don't want to keep everybody waiting.

Jesse: Well, I just wanted to know—can Jared come over to play this afternoon?

Dad: Gosh, Jess—I don't know. I was hoping to take a nap, and I'm not sure what Mom's planning to do. Maybe we can have him over next week.

Jesse: OK…Then can we play catch when we get home—I mean, after you take your nap?

Dad: Sure, but you know your sister will probably want to play, too.

Jesse: Can I still pitch some?

Dad: Just as long as we don't leave Laina out.

Jesse: Great! Thanks! *(Starts to walk away.)*

Dad: Hey, Jess?

(Jesse stops and turns around.)

Dad: Was it hard for you to come and ask me what you could do today?

Jesse: Ha! No, I ask you that stuff all the time. You're my dad. What would be hard about that?

Dad: Well, remember the other night when you said you had a hard time praying?

Jesse: Yeah, I remember.

Dad: Have you ever tried talking to God the way you talk to me?

Jesse: Not really. I mean, I can't see God the way I see you.

Dad: Yeah, that makes it kind of hard. But the next time you pray, try to think of God like you think of me—just your dad. Even though you can't see him.

Jesse: That seems pretty weird, Dad.

Dad: It may seem weird at first, but why don't you give it a try and let me know how it goes, OK? *(Pauses.)* Now you'd better get going. I've got this thing to do.

Jesse: Thanks, Dad!

Dad: *(Pauses, looking up.)* Thanks, Dad!

Discussion Questions:

- What do you think makes it difficult to talk to God as a dad?
- What are the benefits of talking to God as a dad? the dangers?
- Are we free to say anything we feel to God? Why or why not?
- How has your relationship with your dad influenced your view of God?

I Know Something...

Themes: Evangelism, witnessing

Characters: Rex, a no-nonsense middle manager; Pamela, a Christian co-worker

Setting: A typical workplace

Prop: A file folder full of papers

Message: At times Christians make a game out of sharing their faith. Instead of taking the time to earn the right to be heard, we try clever gimmicks to pique people's interest and curiosity. The only problem is that when our presentation of the faith becomes trivial, the world often concludes that our message is trivial, too.

(Pamela approaches Rex from stage left. Rex is looking studiously at papers in a file folder.)

Pamela: *(Playfully)* I know something you don't know.

Rex: Isn't that a little childish, Pamela?

Pamela: I prefer to think of it as playful, if you don't mind. Aren't you going to play along?

Rex: If that's the only way to make you go away, I'll play along.

Pamela: *(Playfully)* I know something you don't know.

Rex: What is it?

Pamela: Guess!

Rex: That's it! I am not interested in playing your silly little game.

Pamela: Oh come on, Rex. You're no fun at all! Can't you even take one guess?

Rex: OK—is this something that has to do with me?

Pamela: Could be.

Rex: Could it be considered a good thing?

Pamela: I would have to say…yes. It *is* a good thing.

Rex: *(With worried excitement)* You heard about the promotion I've been expecting?

Pamela: *(Teasing)* Hmm…Nope—that's not it.

Rex: *(Hopeful)* You got a peek at the raises and bonuses for the year?

Pamela: *(Mockingly)* You're expecting a bonus?

Rex: *(Frustrated)* All right! If this is a good thing and it has to do with me, why don't you just come right out and tell me?

Pamela: What fun would that be? Why should I just blurt out good news when I can make you work for it?

Rex: Because maybe if I have to work for it, I'll lose interest in hearing it at all.

Pamela: But this is really good news for you. Really, really good news.

Rex: It's obviously not that good or you wouldn't play games with it. If it were truly good news, you'd come right out with it.

Pamela: Why? Don't you like playing games?

Rex: Pamela, you don't play games with really good news. Games are for trivia. And since you're being coy with this bit of news, I'm left to assume that it really is trivial. In fact, I'm sure that now, even after I hear it, it won't mean that much to me. See, I'm back where we started. I don't want to play this stupid game with you.

Pamela: But…but…

Rex: But what, Pamela?

Pamela: *(Playfully)* I know something you don't know.

(Rex throws up his hands and walks away.)

Discussion Questions:

● How would you handle the situation differently if you were Pamela?

● What are some of the games Christians play when we share our faith?

● How else do we give non-Christians a negative view of the Christian faith?

● What are effective ways to communicate the gospel? ineffective ways?

Job Security

Themes: Ethics, work and career

Characters: Tim, a conscientious Christian office worker; Earl, a fellow worker with flexible standards

Setting: Tim's office

Props: A small table or desk, a chair, file folders, paperwork, and a telephone

Message: There are many compromises made in the working world. At times these compromises are necessary, but sometimes they're made out of fear—fear of job loss, fear of the boss, and so on. Christians, however, aren't dependent on humans and don't need to compromise in order to keep their favor. Knowing that God provides, we can confidently choose the ethical way at all times.

(Tim is seated center stage at a table or desk. The illusion of office space can be created with file folders, paperwork, and a phone on the table. Earl enters from stage right.)

Earl: Hey, Tim—how's that project going?

Tim: Which project?

Earl: You know, the one you were assigned two weeks ago. The one that you're supposed to present to the top brass next week. The one that's going to earn you a fat raise and a new office.

Tim: *(Unenthusiastically)* Oh, that project.

Earl: Like you didn't know what I was talking about! I know you've been thinking about it. It's the hottest topic on the office grapevine.

Tim: Yeah, you're right. I have been thinking about it *(pausing)* and praying about it and struggling with it and agonizing over it.

Earl: What's the big deal?

Tim: You know that what they want me to do is questionable.

Earl: *(Disbelieving)* Questionable? It's a shrewd business move, one that could position the company to dominate our market. How is it questionable?

Tim: Morally, ethically... in every way except, perhaps, legally.

Earl: I don't know about that, Tim—I think you're overreacting.

Tim: Maybe I am, but I always promised myself that nothing would compromise my Christian ethics, nothing—including my job!

Earl: Well, with that kind of a holier-than-thou attitude, you might just lose your job. There are a lot of people around here who wouldn't think twice about taking on this project.

Tim: I'm not a lot of people, and I don't set my standards by the flow of the crowd. This is a tough decision, but it won't be based on what others would do. I simply don't know if I can make the compromises this project requires.

Earl: But if you don't compromise, you'll give up your job and your salary! You'll be the laughingstock of the entire company. What's worse, you'll make your family suffer, all so you can feel good about yourself. I think you'd better give this some more thought.

Tim: Listen, Earl—I know all kinds of people who are so focused on their jobs and their paychecks that they would do anything to keep them—and I do mean anything. But above all else, my trust is in God. My identity is not wrapped up in my job, and my security isn't based on my paycheck. And by the way, that family comment was a cheap shot. My family trusts me to do what's right, not what's easy.

Earl: So Mr. Fearless can just throw away his career on a whim.

Tim: I didn't say I wasn't afraid. To be honest, I'm so scared that I can't eat or sleep. This is the biggest battle I've ever faced in my working life. My faith is being taken to the limits by my fear. I want to take a stand, but it's hard when the stakes are so high. It feels really lonely to do what you know is right. But this decision is not based on a whim. It's based on a relationship, a relationship I can't replace with a career.

Earl: You amaze me. I mean, I go to church and everything, but I would never let it mess with my life like this. And I don't know too many people who would!

Discussion Questions:

- Which personal standards are you unwilling to compromise? willing to compromise?

- To what extent should we compromise personal standards for the good of others?

- How can we know when we should disobey a human authority in order to obey God?

- What are the dangers of compromising personal beliefs? of never compromising?

Kid Stuff

. . . .

Themes: Bible study, spiritual growth

Characters: Brad, an avid student of the Bible; Tim, a nominal Christian

Setting: The lobby of a church immediately after the worship service

Props: None needed

Message: Many Christian adults feel that they've outgrown the need to study the Bible. They view Bible study as something that children do in Sunday school. However, no one can ever know and understand all the truths that God's Word conveys, so one can never outgrow the need to study the Bible.

(Tim enters from stage left, walking rather briskly. Brad follows and calls to Tim.)

Brad: Tim! Hey, Tim!

Tim: *(Turning to Brad)* Oh—hi, Brad. Were you calling me?

Brad: Yeah, I wanted to catch you before you got out of the building. Where are you headed in such a hurry?

Tim: *(With an edge of sarcasm and stiffly, as though speaking to a child)* Well, I was going out to my car in the parking lot, and then I thought I'd head home.

Brad: *(Ignoring Tim's tone)* Why are you leaving so soon?

Tim: *(With slight irritation)* Soon? It's not soon, Brad. Church is over, and it's about time, too. Did you know we ran five minutes over today? *(Looks at his watch.)*

Brad: Five minutes over what?

Tim: Five minutes over an hour, that's what. I don't have all day to spend here.

Brad: Oh, I'm sorry to hear you say that. I was hoping you would stay for Bible study.

Tim: *(Chuckling)* You're kidding, right? I don't know many people who go to Bible study.

Brad: I know—that's why I wanted to invite you.

Tim: *(With sincerity)* I appreciate the invitation, Brad—really I do. But do you really think I need to go to some remedial class?

Brad: Remedial class? What, exactly, do you mean by that?

Tim: Everyone knows that adult Bible study is a remedial class for people who didn't get it in Sunday school. Bible study is pretty much kid stuff, unless you plan to make a career out of it—like the pastor. Believe me, I'm not into it that much! *(Snickers.)*

Brad: You really believe that Bible study is just for kids? Where in the world did you get that idea?

Tim: Open your eyes, Brad. I've been in lots of churches. Everywhere you see hundreds of kids in Sunday school, vacation Bible school, confirmation classes, and kids clubs, but only a handful of adults trying to catch up in their little Bible study classes. If Bible study isn't primarily for kids, why are they the only ones we make such a fuss about?

Brad: Well, that is a good question, but surely you realize that the church does not believe that Bible study is just for kids.

Tim: If it makes you feel any better, I already know about Adam and Eve, the Fall, the Flood, the Ten Commandments, David and Goliath, Jonah and the big fish, Jesus and the fishermen, the Crucifixion, the Resurrection, the stoning of Paul, *and* the Immaculate Reception.

Brad: *(Incredulously)* What?

Tim: Bible stories, Brad—Bible stories. I heard 'em all when I was a kid. I don't need to hear them again. Now if you don't mind, I have an appointment with a cup of coffee and the Sunday funnies.

Brad: I won't keep you any longer. You're obviously way past kid stuff!

Discussion Questions:

- To what extent do you agree with Brad's statements? disagree with them?
- How do we give the impression that Bible stories are just for kids?
- What are the dangers of not having a regular time of Bible study?
- What can we do to show people the benefits of serious Bible study?

Let Go and Let God

· ·

Themes: Faith, reliance on God

Characters: Brad and Mary; Tim and Kerby—two married couples out on a double date

Setting: The parking lot of a theater following a movie

Props: None needed

Message: God wants us to bring all our needs to him. Unfortunately, we often pick and chose what is "important" enough to bother God with. We need to learn that there is nothing too small or too large for God to be involved with in our lives.

(Both couples walk slowly from stage left toward center stage as they talk.)

Tim: What a great movie!

Mary: I don't know. I thought it was pretty unrealistic.

Tim: Unrealistic! What was unrealistic?

Mary: Well, first of all, in the real world, there's no way he could've gotten away with all that he did. Secondly, if he really were a good guy, he wouldn't have stayed with the firm after he found out what they were doing.

Kerby: I have to agree with Mary. I would have handled the entire situation differently.

Brad: OK—if we're going to talk about realism, what would you do if you found out something illegal was going on at work?

Kerby: Well, the first thing I would do is pray about it.

Tim: Pray about it? As a first option? Maybe eventually, if it was something serious, but...

Mary: Wait a minute—are you saying she shouldn't pray about what happens at work?

Tim: No. I'm saying you don't have to pray about everything. I mean, God expects us to be smart enough to handle some problems on our own. We shouldn't always go whining to him about every little thing.

Brad: You know, you may be right. Taking every little decision to God is probably a waste of time for you *and* for him.

Tim: Hold on, I didn't exactly say *that*. It's just that there are a lot of problems that I can handle on my own. Most solutions are fairly obvious. No sense adding an extra step if you don't have to.

Kerby: Boy, it sounds as though you leave God out of the loop most of the time. Do you really have that narrow of a view of where God can help?

Mary: Lighten up. I'm sure that Tim prays to God more than it seems and has no trouble relying on him.

Tim: Thank you, Mary. You're right, I do trust God. And when I need his help, I know he's there for me. When things get rough and I just can't handle something, I know I can go to him and he'll take care of it.

Brad: You make God sound like the emergency kit I keep in the trunk of my car! I know it's there, but unless I'm in an accident, I'll never need to use it.

Kerby: I agree with Brad. I believe that God is always there for me. So good times or bad, emergency or not, I want to talk to him. I don't want to wait until I'm desperate to talk to him.

Mary: You know, you're right. If you trust that God is always there, why would you want to tackle any situation without him?

Tim: I can see I'm in the minority here, but I still believe that God expects us to handle most problems on our own. I don't think trust has anything to do with it.

Mary: *(Pointing)* Hey, is that a new bumper sticker on your car?

Tim: Yeah! I just bought it. It says, "Let Go and Let God."

(Everyone looks at Tim quizzically.)

Tim: You know... when you have to.

Discussion Questions:

- Which of the four characters do you most identify with and why? least identify with and why?

- Do you think we should pray before buying a new house? a new pair of shoes? Why or why not?

- How should we balance taking responsibility for our own lives and relying completely on God?

- Which is easier for you: to let go and let God or to handle things on your own? How can you better balance the two?

Loving

· · · · · · · · · · · · ·

Themes: Commitment, love

Characters: Scott and Chuck, two friends

Setting: A practice green at a golf course

Props: Two golf putters and two golf balls

Message: Words can lose their meaning when we use them too often or inappropriately. For example, we use the word "love" with reference to so many things that "love" ends up meaning nothing. Although God wants us to understand and experience real love, it's difficult to do when we've lost touch with the real meaning of the word.

(Scott and Chuck are standing center stage. Each has a putter and a golf ball to suggest being on a practice green.)

Chuck: Hey, Scott—did I show you my new putter?

Scott: Yes, Chuck—more than once.

Chuck: Oh...well, I just *love* my new putter.

Scott: Obviously. So what else is new with you?

Chuck: Well, it's late July, and you know what that means—preseason football! I *love* football! I can hardly wait!

Scott: So, do you think the Bears *(or a local football team)* have any chance at all this year?

Chuck: It's hard to tell. Doesn't matter though—I just *love* the Bears, no matter what. Hey, have you checked out my car?

49

Scott: Sure, I've seen your car. Or did you get a new car lately?

Chuck: No. I just spent some time cleaning my old one up, and it looks great! I washed it, waxed it, rubbed it down with Armor All...I just *love* my car!

Scott: I don't mean to be rude, Chuck, but either you are the most loving person in the history of the universe or you don't know what love is at all.

Chuck: What makes you say that?

Scott: Well, so far you've told me that you love your putter, that you love football (particularly the Bears), and that you love your car.

Chuck: So what's your point? Are you saying that I don't love all those things?

Scott: What I'm saying is that maybe you should think about what you mean when you claim to love something. I mean, what is love to you?

Chuck: You want me to explain love to you? OK—I'll tell you what love is... *(With a look of recognition)* Wait a minute! You're just pulling my leg. You had me going there for a minute. Scott, you have such a dry sense of humor. I *love* that about you.

Scott: There you go again with that love business. It's starting to drive me crazy!

Chuck: Really, you can stop now. I get the joke. I have to tell you, Scott, I *really* love you.

Scott: That means a lot to me, Chuck...coming from you.

Discussion Questions:

- How would you explain love to a five-year-old? to your spouse? to a non-Christian?

- How is loving a thing different from loving a person? In what ways are they the same?

- When has someone treated you like a thing? When have you treated others like things?

- Without saying "I love you," how will you speak or show love to someone this week?

Our Little Secret

· ·

Themes: Evangelism, witnessing

Characters: Miss Tellefsen, a Christian public school teacher; C.J., a student in her class who attends the same church as Miss Tellefsen

Setting: Miss Tellefsen's classroom after school

Props: A small table or desk, a chair, several school books, and an "in" tray

Message: Sharing our faith in Jesus can be difficult, particularly when it's unpopular or illegal to do so. But even when we can demonstrate our faith, we sometimes make excuses to avoid doing so. We even go so far as to hide our faith from others for fear of what they might think or do. However, since we have the best news any one could ever hear, we shouldn't keep it a secret.

(Miss Tellefsen is seated at her desk. Place school books and an "in" tray on the desk or table to suggest a classroom teacher's space.)

C.J.: *(Entering from stage left)* Miss Tellefsen?

Miss Tellefsen: Hi, C.J.—can I help you?

C.J.: I hope so. I wanted to talk to you about class.

Miss Tellefsen: If you're concerned about your grade, I can tell you right now that there's nothing to worry about. You're a very good student, and I enjoy having you in my class.

C.J.: No. It's not my grade. I'm not having any problems that way. It's . . . *(pauses uncomfortably.)*

Miss Tellefsen: It's OK, C.J.—tell me what's on your mind.

C.J.: You see, I know that you go to my church. I see you there, and I know you see me because you said "hi" to me once.

Miss Tellefsen: Well, that's really not a secret. We do go to the same church, and I do see you there quite often. I guess I don't say "hi" much because I figure you see me so often at school that you might like a break on weekends. Are you hurt that I don't say "hi" more often?

C.J.: *(Nervously)* No, not at all. Actually, I'm kind of glad because I'd feel like we'd have to talk every week, and we do see enough of each other here at school. *(Pauses and takes a deep breath.)* What's bothering me is that we both go to church on Sunday, but during the week, we don't talk about it. I mean, I never hear you talk about Jesus in class, and I hardly ever talk about Jesus with my friends.

Miss Tellefsen: Why do you think that is? Are you ashamed of Jesus or of going to church?

C.J.: No! A lot of my friends go to church—we just don't talk about it. Are you ashamed of Jesus?

Miss Tellefsen: *(Defensively)* Not at all. It's something completely different for me. It's against the law for me to talk about Jesus in class.

C.J.: Against the law? Are you serious?

Miss Tellefsen: Actually, there are certain ways I could share my faith with students. I guess I'm just afraid of crossing the line and upsetting someone.

C.J.: You mean upsetting people who could fire you?

Miss Tellefsen: Yes. Upsetting people like that. So I play it safe and don't really say anything in class.

C.J.: But it's not illegal to talk about Jesus with the other teachers or with friends, is it?

Miss Tellefsen: No. I could do that more often...except I sometimes feel uncomfortable pushing my beliefs on other people. *(Abruptly shifting focus)* What about you? What keeps you from speaking up?

C.J.: Mostly I'm afraid my friends won't hang around with me if I start talking about Jesus. I wouldn't want them thinking I'm some kind of religious fanatic!

Miss Tellefsen: So you see, I could lose my job and you could lose your friends if we started talking about our faith in Jesus whenever we felt like it.

C.J.: So I guess we should just keep it our little secret?

Miss Tellefsen: *(Nodding and speaking with reluctance)* Perhaps that would be best. *(She looks down and away toward audience, troubled.)*

Discussion Questions:

- How would you respond if you were in Miss Tellefsen's situation? C.J.'s situation?

- How might Miss Tellefsen share her faith without breaking the law or offending others?

- What makes it difficult for you to share your faith in Jesus as freely as you should?

- What can you do this week to get ready to share your faith? to actually share it?

Please Don't Let Me Be Misunderstood

....

Themes: Communication, theological disagreements

Characters: Kerby and Rex, members of the drama team; Tim, the drama director; Brad, the worship leader

Setting: A rehearsal for the Sunday drama

Props: Four copies of the drama script

Message: Communication is tricky. Sometimes we may think we're looking at the same thing as another person, but we actually have two different sets of information. On the other hand, even when we're looking at identical information, we sometimes see and understand it differently. This happens often with Scripture. Everyone has the same Bible, yet there are many different views on what it actually says. To avoid miscommunication, we need to make sure that we're all "reading from the same page" and actually listening to what other people are saying.

(Rex and Kerby stand center stage. Each is holding a script. Tim and Brad are seated in the front row, watching and following along with their scripts.)

Rex: Hi, Kerby.

Kerby: I'm having a wonderful weekend.

Rex: *(A little confused)* I don't think I asked you about your weekend.

Kerby: Well, I hope everything is going well with you, too.

Rex: Things would be going much better if your responses made some sense to me.

Kerby: *(Trying diligently to stick to the script)* Thank you very much, but I'm going to be busy most of this week.

Rex: *(Obviously abandoning his script)* Hold it, hold it. Something has gone terribly wrong here. Maybe we should start this conversation over.

Kerby: *(Still not catching on)* That sounds like fun to me, but do you think everyone will be interested in going?

Tim: *(Walking up to center stage)* Wait a minute, you two. Didn't you get the script I prepared for the sermon? Brad, come here a minute.

Brad: What's wrong, Tim?

Tim: Do you have the script I wrote for this sketch?

Brad: Yeah, it's right here. I got my copy last Wednesday.

Tim: Great! Would you please check Rex's script?

(Rex hands his script to Brad.)

Tim: Here, Kerby—*(taking her script)* let me check your script.

Brad: Rex's script is the same as mine.

Tim: And Kerby's is identical to mine. The opening line is, "Hey, Kerby—how's your weekend going?"

Brad: Actually, Rex's script starts out with, "Hi, Kerby."

Tim: Wait a minute. Those aren't the same opening lines. Let me see that script. *(He looks at Rex's copy.)* I think there's been a mistake.

Brad: What was your first clue, Einstein? How could you possibly give two people two different scripts for the same drama on the same day?

Tim: Sorry—I was playing around with two different concepts. I was running late this week, and I must have run two different copies and handed them both out. I *am* sorry, you guys. I hope you'll forgive the misunderstanding.

Brad: At least we caught it at rehearsal before everybody in church saw it.

(Tim and Brad return to their seats in the front row.)

Rex: Well, I'm glad we got that straightened out.

Kerby: So am I. Imagine, two different scripts for the same day. I was willing to play along, but I'm glad Tim stopped us before we made fools of ourselves with that ridiculous misunderstanding.

Rex: *(Thoughtfully)* Maybe this is like what happened to Jesus.

Kerby: Here we go again. What exactly do you mean by that?

Rex: I'm sorry, I really don't want to be misunderstood again. What I mean is that Jesus butted heads with the religious leaders of his day. Maybe it's because Jesus was using a different script. And when they couldn't understand what he was saying, they just kept reading from their script and getting angry when it didn't match his.

Kerby: That's an interesting thought, Rex—and for once, I actually understand what you're saying.

Rex: Well, that's because we're finally on the same page!

Kerby: *(Playfully reading from her script)* I'm having a wonderful weekend.

Rex: *(Also playfully)* Kerby, I don't think I asked you about your weekend!

Discussion Questions:

- What did the religious leaders of Jesus' day expect of the Messiah? Why did they expect that?

- What do you think today's religious leaders would expect of Jesus? Why would they expect that?

- What do you expect Jesus to do for you? to ask of you? Upon what are you basing your expectations?

- What are some disagreements Christians have about what the Bible says? What causes these disagreements?

Resting Comfortably

· ·

Themes: Discipleship, laziness, spiritual growth

Characters: Dan, a high school senior; Tim, an adult friend of the family

Setting: Dan's backyard

Prop: A reclining lawn chair

Message: God has given us everything we need in Jesus. Unfortunately, sometimes people use this as an excuse to keep from taking responsibility for their lives. However, we are not to lie around waiting for Christ's return. Our relationship with Christ carries with it a responsibility to serve him.

(Dan is relaxing in a reclining lawn chair as Tim enters from stage left.)

Tim: Hi, Dan. Looks like you're resting comfortably.

Dan: Yep! Nice day, warm sun—there's no place I'd rather be.

Tim: I can certainly relate to that. Say, is your dad around?

Dan: Nope. He went in to the office to catch up on some paperwork.

Tim: That's too bad. I can think of better ways to spend a Saturday afternoon. *(Pauses.)* By the way, how are those college plans coming?

Dan: Oh, I don't think I'm going.

Tim: *(Surprised)* You don't think you're going? After all that time you spent comparing schools and all the agonizing you went through trying to pick just the right one?

Dan: It has been pretty tough. *(Pauses.)* I *did* get accepted to a couple of schools, though.

Tim: But you're not going to any of them?

Dan: Nope.

Tim: *(Pauses.)* So where will you be working?

Dan: What?

Tim: *(With minor frustration)* I said, where will you be working?

Dan: I don't think I'll be working anywhere.

Tim: That's too bad. No one's called back?

Dan: Called back from where?

Tim: From your job interviews.

Dan: Oh, I haven't had any job interviews.

Tim: Let me get this straight. You aren't going to college, you don't have a job, and you're not planning to look for a job.

Dan: Right on all counts!

Tim: Then my only question is—how are you going to get by? Who's going to pay for your food and clothing?

Dan: That's easy. My dad said he'd take care of me.

Tim: *(Amused)* Oh, really? And when did he say that?

Dan: My entire life. Lucky for me, I remembered it before I went to all the trouble of college or work. See, everything's going to be great.

Tim: Dan, have you checked this out with your dad lately?

Dan: No need! He's been telling me for years that he would take care of me, and I take him at his word.

Tim: Dan, speaking as a father myself, I'm sure your dad loves you very much, and I'm sure he's promised to take care of you. But I think he would be more than a little surprised at your interpretation of his promise.

Dan: You mean he expects me to go to college and get a job?

Tim: Does that surprise you? Did you really think he was going to cater to your every need?

Dan: Well, of course! He said he'd always take care of me.

Tim: And you can rest comfortably knowing he will support you as much as he can. At the same time, I suspect he also expects you to take responsibility for your life and to use your abilities to do what you can.

Dan: Well, that isn't at all the comfortable rest I had in mind!

Discussion Questions:

- To what extent does God want us to rest comfortably in him? to take responsibility for our lives?

- What are the dangers of resting completely in God? of assuming responsibility for our own lives?

- Which is hardest for you: to take responsibility for your own life or to rely completely on God? Why?

- What is one thing you can do this week to trust God more? to take more responsibility for your life?

Something of Consequence

. . . .

Themes: Frustration, joy, peace

Characters: Katherine, who is peaceful and upbeat;
Mike, who is edgy and irritable

Setting: A chance meeting between friends

Props: None needed

Message: When we base our contentment or satisfaction
on the behavior of others, we're destined for frustration.
Lasting peace and joy can only be found in a relationship with Jesus Christ. Every other source of stability
and satisfaction will eventually fail us.

*(Katherine enters from stage right as Mike enters from stage left. Just as they cross
center stage, the conversation begins.)*

Mike: Hey, Katherine—where have you been lately? I haven't seen you in weeks.

Katherine: Oh, I've been around. I guess we've just been missing each other.

Mike: So—how have you been?

Katherine: Great! Things couldn't be better.

Mike: You know, it's true what they say. Some things never change.

Katherine: What do you mean by that?

Mike: Well, every time I see you you're upbeat. Not always happy or jolly,
but...up. The strangest thing about it is that it seems genuine.

Katherine: Since when did being genuine become strange?

Mike: Being genuine isn't strange, but you have to admit that being genuinely upbeat all the time is unusual. Doesn't anything bad ever happen to you?

Katherine: Of course it does! Just yesterday, I put a rock through my radiator, and now my car is in the shop. It's going to cost me a pretty penny to get it fixed, too. And last week I found out that my company is downsizing, so I may be looking for work soon.

Mike: Wait a minute, wait a minute. You just said you've been great and that things couldn't be better.

Katherine: So?

Mike: So? *(A little bewildered)* So, were you simply making polite conversation? It sure doesn't sound like things are great.

Katherine: Oh, there's always stuff going on in my life. Some of it's a lot of fun, and some is a real pain. But it's still just stuff.

Mike: I get it, the old "stuff happens" routine. Bad stuff can happen to you, but you never have a bad day.

Katherine: I didn't say that. Of course I have bad days. In fact, I'm not thrilled that my car is in the shop. It's just that my attitude toward the day isn't determined by how my car runs.

Mike: I get furious when my car breaks down. I'm almost ashamed to admit it, but once it died in traffic, and I got so mad that I punched out the windshield. Then I had two problems on my hands.

Katherine: To be perfectly honest, Mike, I've seen you go ballistic about some pretty ridiculous things.

Mike: Like what?

Katherine: Like the time you thought the store clerk chatted too long with the woman in front of you. I was afraid you were going to start throwing things.

Mike: I was in a hurry that day. He should have seen that I was in a rush.

Katherine: OK—how about that time the teenager in the car ahead of us threw a candy wrapper out the window? You chased him a mile and a half, flashing your lights and honking your horn the entire way. You even passed our exit.

Mike: I just can't tolerate littering.

Katherine: Then there was that time you demanded that the management throw that guy off the golf course because he . . .

Mike: OK, OK—enough already. What's your point?

Katherine: Well, I can say that I'm great when I have bad stuff going on in my life because I'm not looking for my joy or contentment to come from stuff out there.

Mike: Out where?

Katherine: Out there ... from other people, from things, from personal accomplishments.

Mike: Then where in the world do you get your joy?

Katherine: From the only thing that never breaks down, rusts, rots, or goes away!

Mike: Which is?

Katherine: Knowing that God's love for me never changes. That's something that pretty much makes everything else inconsequential.

Mike: I guess I can't argue with you there!

Discussion Questions:

● What kinds of people or situations frustrate you most? Why do they frustrate you?

● What is your greatest source of joy? What is it about this that brings you such joy?

● How would you respond if you suddenly lost your job? the person you most love?

● What specific steps can you take to increase your faith in God? to prepare for loss?

Taking the Day Off

. . . .

Themes: Responsibility, work and career

Characters: Nick, a responsible store clerk; Matt, an irresponsible co-worker

Setting: The break room at a retail electronics store

Props: None needed

Message: Although God wants us to enjoy life, we're also expected to live responsibly. We shouldn't get caught up in a selfish lifestyle that disregards the needs of others. When we abuse our God-given freedom, we often hurt others without even realizing it.

Production note: There should be a "youthful" feel to this drama, so you may want to have both characters played by "twenty-somethings."

(Nick and Matt are standing center stage. We join the conversation in progress.)

Matt: Hey, Nick—want to go down to the beach tomorrow? It's gonna be a beautiful day.

Nick: I'd love to, Matt—except we have one annoying little problem.

Matt: What's that?

Nick: We have to work tomorrow.

Matt: Not me—I'm calling in sick. I wouldn't pass up a gorgeous day, especially this late in the summer.

Nick: Didn't you call in sick last week?

Matt: Yeah, I guess I did.

Nick: Were you really sick then?

Matt: Sort of. I was up late the night before, and I just couldn't drag myself out of bed!

Nick: I hate to break it to you, buddy—you've got to get a handle on things.

Matt: All right, all right. So don't come to the beach tomorrow! I didn't know you were so against having a good time.

Nick: That's not fair. You know as well as anyone that I'm not against having a good time. It's more about when having a good time is good for you. Quite frankly, I think you need to pace yourself a little.

Matt: Well, I say, *"carpe diem*—seize the day!" I'm not going to miss the end of summer sitting in some boring store.

Nick: So it doesn't bother you that you'll be letting down everyone in our department?

Matt: It's just one day, Nick. It's not the end of the world. I'm sure everyone will get by just fine.

Nick: Actually, it's a lot more than one day. It's your whole attitude, and it's starting to get to everyone. You don't see it because you're never around, but even the people who like you are affected. They make excuses for your behavior, but it's starting to cause a lot of friction in the store. You know, everyone respected you when you started, but now... well, I'm not so sure.

Matt: That's their problem. There is nothing wrong with being out where the fun is. I don't see how I'm hurting anyone else. So come tomorrow, I am outta here.

Nick: No need to wait till tomorrow. You're already outta control!

Matt: *(With a celebrative whoop)* Yeah! *(He furrows his brow as he realizes it was not a compliment.)*

Discussion Questions:

- Which of these two characters do you most identify with? Why?
- How do you think God feels about us taking time simply to relax?
- What are the dangers of working too much? of relaxing too much?
- What principles might help us know when to work? when to relax?

The Bright Side of Death

· · · · · · · · · · · · · · · ·

Themes: Comfort, death, eternal life

Characters: Tim, the drama director; Rex, a drama-team member

Setting: A worship preparation meeting

Props: None needed

Message: Most people have a difficult time dealing with death, so they avoid any mention of its reality. However, the church is one place where death can be handled with comfort and even joy. Because we know the hope of eternal life with Jesus Christ, we can help people look past their dark fears to the bright side of death.

(Tim is standing center stage, and he calls Rex out of his place in the front row of the congregation.)

Tim: Rex, I think I've finally reached my creative limits. I don't think I have any skits left in me.

Rex: What are you talking about?

Tim: Did you see the topic for this week's message?

Rex: Sure. What about it?

Tim: Death, Rex. The topic is death. You know I'm expected to write a sketch that ties to each week's topic. How in the world can I write a skit about death?

Rex: I don't know… but I'm sure you'll, uh, dig something up.

Tim: Very funny! You see, that's exactly my problem. I can't go out there and joke about death, so my sketch can't be humorous.

Rex: Why not?

Tim: Death can be a very difficult subject for people to deal with. If we make light of it, we'll be bound to hurt someone's feelings. You know someone in the congregation will be grieving the recent death of a parent or a spouse or, God forbid, a child!

Rex: Yeah, I see your point. So take a more serious approach.

Tim: Right. Get myself worked up, do several minutes of heavy-duty grieving, and have everyone in tears. That's a wonderful formula for Sunday morning!

Rex: I wasn't suggesting that it be *that* serious.

Tim: Listen, Rex—there's just no easy answer here. The best thing for everyone would be for us to skip this topic altogether. Our message is one of life and light and the joy of the gospel. Why in the world do we have to talk about death in church?

Rex: Because there's something else that's just as true and real as the gospel.

Tim: What's that?

Rex: Death, Tim. None of us gets out of this alive! Death is inevitable, the natural end to life.

Tim: I'm not arguing that. My point is simply that death seems to be an awfully touchy topic for Sunday morning. And it's doubly difficult to treat it properly in a brief sketch!

Rex: Actually, I can't think of a better place to talk about death. I don't know of any other place where death can be talked about in a positive light. Your drama could reflect that!

Tim: I appreciate your attempt to help me past my writer's block, but isn't it a bit too much to try to talk about death in a positive light?

Rex: Not at all. In the church we can talk about death with hope and comfort. Better yet, we can talk about victory. In fact, this could be a very upbeat topic.

Tim: Death as an upbeat topic? Who in the world is going to buy that?

Rex: Anyone who has the hope of eternal life with Jesus Christ!

Discussion Questions:

- What is the most difficult death you have had to face? What made it so difficult?

- What is the most difficult death you might face? What would make it so difficult?

- What scares you most about dying? How can God help you overcome those fears?

- What can God do to help us face the death of a loved one? How can we help each other?

This Is My Dad

· ·

Themes: Father's Day, parenting

Characters: Voice 1, a young boy of perhaps six or seven; Voice 2, a young girl of about the same age; Voice 3, a preteen boy; Voice 4, a teenage girl; Voice 5, a teenage boy; Voice 6, an adult male; Voice 7, an adult female

Setting: This drama is performed with an empty stage and offstage voices. Set a silhouette cutout of a male figure in the center of the stage. This figure will represent "Dad" as the voices speak.

Prop: A silhouette cutout of a male figure (You can cut the figure out of heavy cardboard. Attach a long, wooden dowel to the back of the figure to hold it up.)

Message: This is a reflective piece about fathers. It spans the ages of life we spend with our fathers and is designed to help people reflect on their experiences with their fathers.

Production note: You may want to prerecord all the voices so you can capture the right mood and intensity. Be sure to use a high-quality tape and tape recorder for best sound reproduction. The other option is to have all the voices use an offstage microphone.

(The Dad silhouette cutout is placed center stage.)

Voice 1: This is my dad. He's the best. He takes me fishing and plays with me in the backyard. At night he reads me stories before bedtime. I like it when I sit on his lap and he gives me big hugs. This is my dad.

Voice 2: This is my dad. He's funny. Even when I feel like crying, he can make me laugh. He takes me to the park and gives me "underdogs" on the swings. Last month we went to a father-daughter dance together. I don't think he wanted to go, but we had lots of fun. I like the way he scratches my cheek with his whiskers. This is my dad.

Voice 3: This is my dad. He likes to tease me, and sometimes he doesn't know when to quit. When I get upset, he feels bad, and we talk. Sometimes I think he understands me, but other times I'm not so sure. He's still pretty cool even if he does embarrass me in front of my friends. This is my dad.

Voice 4: This is my dad. He doesn't live with us any longer. He and Mom couldn't seem to get along. I see him every weekend . . . when he remembers to come and pick me up. It's not that he doesn't care—I think he just forgets. He's a very busy man. He's always been busy, even when he lived with us. I wish we could spend more time together. This is my dad.

Voice 5: This is my dad. We've always had a great time together. I remember when he coached my first Little League team. My friends thought he played favorites, but I knew he was being fair. I'm older now, and sometimes we don't get along. It's not that we don't love each other. He says he's afraid of losing me. Soon I'll be moving out and going away to college. I know things have to change, but some things will always stay the same. This is my dad.

Voice 6: This is my dad. He died when I was seventeen years old. It's strange how a person can become a concept over time. I mean, I get a strange feeling when I see guys my age interacting with their fathers and I have no idea how they must feel. I tell myself that in some ways I'm fortunate. I'll never have to watch my dad get old. I won't have to make those difficult decisions about nursing homes and long-term care. My dad will always be exactly as he was when I was seventeen. I tell myself that . . . and on good days, I believe it. This is my dad.

Voice 7: This is my dad. He's older now and not as strong as I remember. One thing's for sure, though—he has gotten smarter and smarter over the past twenty years. I distinctly remember when my dad suddenly increased in wisdom. It was about three months after the birth of my first child. I know the day is coming when I will have to say goodbye. That word comes with great fear. It's one of those facts of life that everyone wishes was fiction. I don't know how much longer we will have together, and I wish my schedule allowed me to spend more time with him. What I wouldn't give for one more chance to sit on his lap and feel his whiskers on my cheek. This is my dad.

(Allow a moment of silence for the audience to reflect on their fathers.)

Discussion Questions:

- What is your favorite memory of your dad? your strongest memory? your most recent memory?

- If you were to describe your father to someone who didn't know him, what would you say?

- What is one thing you appreciate about your dad? What can you do to show your appreciation?

- How has your relationship with your dad changed over the years? How can you make it better?

While It Was Still Dark

. . . .

Themes: Easter, Good Friday, resurrection

Characters: Mary, one of Jesus' followers; Offstage Voice, preferably a deep male voice

Setting: Mary is alone on stage with no particular place defined

Props: None needed

Message: The followers of Jesus were devastated by his death. Unaware that he would be raised in several days, they became incredibly sad. In this drama, Mary is in a state of denial, still making plans for all that she wants to do with Jesus. She's unwilling to acknowledge his death.

Production note: If your church does not have the lighting capabilities called for in this skit, simply darken the room and use dim lighting on the stage area.

(Mary stands center stage with a pin spotlight on her.)

Mary: It has been so wonderful following him around these past few years. His teaching, his stories, all the wonderful things he did to help people. Mostly his smile. Oh, how I loved to see him smile.

Voice: Mary… he's dead.

(All stage lights begin to dim.)

Mary: *(Shaking her head as if to deny this truth)* When he smiled, or better yet, when he laughed, there was so much joy I was convinced that all of us around him would sprout wings and fly.

Voice: Mary...he's dead.

(Lights dim again.)

Mary: *(Growing angry)* That simply cannot be. He is the Messiah. We are his people. And there is so very much to be done. So you see, he simply cannot be gone. Later this week, we will travel to Galilee and take up where we left off. Word has spread, you see, and people are expecting us. There will be healings and teachings and laughter...so much laughter.

Voice: Mary...he's dead.

(Lights dim further.)

Mary: *(Ignoring the voice with determination in her own voice)* I spoke to a woman just yesterday. Her husband is in failing health. I assured her that Jesus could heal him in an instant. She was so very thankful. I think that will be our first stop on our way back home.

Voice: Mary...he's dead.

(All stage lights except for the pin spotlight on Mary dim further.)

Mary: *(Pleading)* That just isn't so. I saw the crowds only a week ago. They adored him. They spread their coats before him and made such a noise that the whole city wondered what was happening. Things don't change that quickly. I will not believe that it has ended so swiftly, so brutally. The world cannot be without the love of that man.

Voice: Mary...

Mary: *(Sharply)* Enough! I will not hear you again. I know what I saw with my own eyes. Yet I pray that my eyes deceived me. If what I saw was real, then there is no hope for this world. I can't bear to live in a world without hope. Without love. Without him.

Voice: Jesus is dead.

(All lights except the dim pin spotlight on Mary fade to black.)

Mary: And I must go and tend to his body.

Voice: Mary...it is still dark.

Mary: *(Full of pain and sorrow, yet beyond tears)* Yes, it is dark. And I fear that it will be dark for a very, very long time.

(Full blackout for twenty seconds.)

Pastor: But Jesus is risen! He is risen indeed!

(Lights up to full.)

Production note: This drama could also be followed by an explosion of music and singing as the lights come up to full.

Discussion Questions:

- When have you felt as hopeless as Mary? How did you (or could you) overcome those feelings?

- Why do you think God allows people who love him to go through "hopeless" situations?

- How can knowing that Jesus rose from the dead help you face your own hopeless situations?

- How should knowing that Jesus rose from the dead affect the way we live our daily lives?

Wish List

· · · · · · · · · · · · · · · · · · ·

Theme: Prayer

Characters: Kerby, a devout Christian; Brad, a friend from church

Setting: The study room in the church

Props: A small note pad and a pencil

Message: All too often people treat prayer like a shopping list. They fill their prayers with requests and demands and then judge God's love and faithfulness by how they perceive his response. However, prayer is not about what we want from God. It's our recognition of him and what he has already done for us. Prayer is our connection to God so that we will never forget his grace, mercy, and guidance.

(Kerby is standing center stage, checking off "prayer requests" on her note pad. She should be turned slightly away from Brad when he enters.)

Kerby: *(With great concentration)* Let's see now—I got that, did that, have that...

Brad: Hi, Kerby. What are you doing?

Kerby: *(Slightly startled)* Oh—hi, Brad. I'm just reviewing my prayer list.

Brad: Reviewing your prayer list?

Kerby: Yes, I heard once that you appreciate God so much more when you keep track of what you pray for and occasionally look back to see how God has answered your prayers.

Brad: I've heard of people reviewing their prayer lists, but did I hear you say "appreciate God"?

Kerby: Yes. You know, when you look back and see all the great stuff that you get when you go to God, you really start to appreciate him.

Brad: I don't mean to offend you, Kerby, but you sort of make God sound like the Home Shopping Network and prayer as his 800 number!

Kerby: Are you saying that I shouldn't pray to God when I have needs or I want something done? Are you implying that I shouldn't rely on God for my needs?

Brad: *(Gently)* No, I'm not suggesting that at all. Of course you should pray, but listen to yourself for a moment: "I need ... I want ... my needs ..." Do you hear a pattern here?

Kerby: I'm sorry, Brad, but you're confusing me. On the one hand, you say I should pray to God when I have needs—and I do! But in the same breath you seem to imply that I'm self-centered. How can I pray for what I need without being self-centered?

Brad: Kerby, you need to remember that you are praying to *the* holy God. Prayer isn't simply about what you want *from* him; it's also about what he wants *for* you. Prayer is about recognizing who he is and where you fit in his plan. It seems to me that you have a tidy plan already in place and you want God to fit into it!

Kerby: So you're saying that prayer is more about God than it is about me.

Brad: No! I'm saying that prayer is all about God. Don't you get it? God has a plan for you. He has gifted you, he has challenged you, and he has given you prayer as a way to sort out who you are and where you fit in his plan. I like to pray, "Lord, what are you teaching me?" It gives me perspective.

Kerby: So I guess I don't need to keep track of my prayers and how they're answered anymore. That's what I get for listening to bad advice!

Brad: Don't get me wrong, Kerby. Keeping track of your prayers is a great idea. I love seeing how God's plan for my life is unfolding, but the only way I can see it is through hindsight. Looking back increases my faith in God and what he has in store for me.

Kerby: Wow! I guess I *have* been treating my prayer list like a wish list and grading God on his performance. But didn't the pastor say that we're supposed to call on God like we would our dad? "Abba" means "Daddy." I know I heard that right.

Brad: And that's the greatest part. The holy God invites us to get that close to him. But, Kerby, it's Daddy—not Father Christmas!

Discussion Questions:

- When you pray, do you tend to focus more on what God wants or on what you want?

- How fully do you agree that prayer is *all* about God? How might you reword this statement?

- How can we cultivate a spirit of thanks without treating God like Father Christmas?

- How should our prayers reflect that fact that God is our Father? that God is holy?

Topical Index

● ●

Evaluation of *SERMON-BOOSTER DRAMAS*

Please help Group Publishing, Inc., continue to provide innovative and usable resources for ministry by taking a moment to fill out and send us this evaluation. Thanks!

● ● ●

1. As a whole, this book has been (circle one):

　　Not much help　　　　　　　　　　　　　　　　　Very helpful

　　1　　2　　3　　4　　5　　6　　7　　8　　9　　10

2. The things I liked best about this book were:

3. This book could be improved by:

4. I would like a second volume of dramas to address the following themes:

5. Optional Information:

　　Name _____

　　Street Address _____

　　City _____ State _____ Zip _____

　　Phone Number _____ Date _____

More Practical Resources for Your Adult Ministry

You Can Double Your Class in Two Years or Less
Josh Hunt

No pie-in-the-sky theories or suggestions of what *should* work here. Author Josh Hunt has tested the strategies for growth presented here in the real world of church boards and busy neighborhoods...and his suggestions *work*.

Here is a clear vision...a practical plan for getting the job done...and a specific, measurable goal: doubling any adult class or group.

Pastors, leaders of adult Sunday school classes, and anyone else who's tired of *talking about* growth and wants to see it *happen* will find this book irresistible—and well worth the modest investment.

ISBN 0-7644-2019-4

Bore No More!
(For Every Pastor, Speaker, Teacher)
Mike & Amy Nappa

These 70 audience-grabbing ideas pull listeners into your sermon or lesson—and drive your message home!

Discover clever object lessons, creative skits, and readings. Music and celebration ideas. Affirmation activities. All the innovative techniques **85% of adult churchgoers say they wish their pastors would try during sermons!** (Group Publishing poll)

Involve your congregation in the learning process! These complete 5- to 15-minute activities highlight common New Testament Lectionary passages, so you'll use this book Sunday after Sunday.

ISBN 1-55945-266-8

The Simple Truth: A Bare Bones Bible
Walter Wangerin Jr.

Three hours. That's all it takes to enjoy best-selling author Walter Wangerin Jr.'s delightful retelling of God's Word. In just three hours you'll experience a complete retelling of the Bible in plain, everyday language.

Simple. Compelling. Refreshing. **The Simple Truth: A Bare Bones Bible** paints a portrait of Bible events that's so vivid you'll *experience* them in a fresh, invigorating new way.

The Simple Truth: A Bare Bones Bible is the perfect introductory Bible for new Christians...a life-changing gift for seekers...and a welcome perspective for veteran Bible students. Ideal for youth and adults!

Hardcover   1-55945-630-2
Softcover   1-55945-631-0

Available at your local Christian bookstore or directly from Group Publishing, P.O. Box 485, Loveland, CO 80539.